**Walt Disney**

| DATE DUE | | | |
|---|---|---|---|
| | | | |
| | | | |
| | | | |
| | | | |
| | | | |
| | | | |
| | | | |
| | | | |
| | | | |
| | | | |
| | | | |
| | | | |

**921**
**DISNEY**

Fisher, Maxine P.

**3930013599**

Walt Disney.

**PRAIRIE VIEW JUNIOR HIGH**
**TINLEY PARK IL 60477**

# Walt Disney

## By Maxine P. Fisher

Franklin Watts
New York/London/Toronto/Sydney 1988
A First Book

Flip book drawings by © Michael Sporn Animation, Inc.

Diagram by Vantage Art, Inc.

All photographs courtesy of Walt Disney Company except:
Culver Pictures, Inc.: pp. 8, 44 (top); Kit Hawkins: p. 25 (all three).


Library of Congress Cataloging-in-Publication Data

Fisher, Maxine P., 1948-
Walt Disney / Maxine P. Fisher.

    p.    cm. — (A First book)
Bibliography: p.
Includes index.
Summary: Follows the life and dreams of the Missouri boy who became
a pioneer in the field of cartoon animation as well as bringing
the world live-action films, wildlife documentaries, and amusement parks.
ISBN 0-531-10493-1
1. Disney, Walt, 1901-1966—Juvenile literature.  2. Animators—
United States—Biography—Juvenile literature.  [1. Disney, Walt,
1901-1966.  2. Motion pictures—Biography.]  I. Title.
NC1766.U52D536   1988
791.43′092′4—dc19                                    87-27902   CIP   AC
[B]
[92]

# Contents

For Michael

The flip book drawings that appear in the bottom right hand corners of the right hand pages of this book are from Michael Sporn's animated film, *The Hunting of the Snark*.

Many warm thanks to John Canemaker, Michael Sporn, and David Smith for reading the manuscript.

# 1

# The Perfect Place

Close your eyes and imagine the perfect place. What does it look like? Who is there? Who isn't there? What happens there? How is it different from where you live now? If you ask some of your friends these questions and compare answers, you will probably discover that your imaginary places are somewhat different, and yet in other ways they are the same.

Throughout the ages, people have been dreaming of their perfect places. Some people have done more than just dream; they have worked to make their dream places real. In our century, Walt Disney was such a person. He dreamed and then spent his entire life creating a place that was cosier, safer, and happier than the world we live in.

His name is often linked with the word *magic*. But if you watch the Disney films closely, you will realize that magic alone doesn't make that world cosy and safe. The heroes and heroines of Disney's movies are saved from ruin by some wonderful character or characters whom we admire and cheer for. The dwarfs shelter the stray Snow White. Jiminy Cricket and the Blue Fairy watch over and guide

9

Pinocchio. Timothy Mouse befriends the friendless elephant, Dumbo. Three grandmotherly fairies raise Sleeping Beauty. And Cinderella is helped by the mice who live in her floorboards.

In Disney's world, love and friendship always triumph over meanness and greed. And it's easy to recognize the villains, who are often shown as witchy-looking adults, as well as the good, friendly helpers, who are usually adorable, cuddly animals. Also, unlike in the real world, good is always rewarded in the end and evil is punished.

No one who dreams of such a world is alone; Walt Disney's films have appealed and continue to appeal to millions of people, not only in America but around the world. These films and the characters created for them made Walt Disney a rich man. But the reason for his success lies only partly in the stories and characters. Walt Disney was also a lucky man who twice happened to be on the spot when important technological changes were about to take place in the movie business. He was wise enough to see the future of sound and color for filmmaking. And he was shrewd enough to make deals that enabled him to become a pioneer in the movie industry.

In the last fifteen years of his life, Walt Disney's interest shifted away from film. More than ever before, he wanted to create his perfect place in the real world rather than just on the screen. Being a businessman, he did not build a private pleasure ground, but rather one open to paying customers. He spared no expense in the planning of his park to make it a place that was—and still is—charming, sparkling clean, safe, and comfortable, much like the world of his films, and one that millions of people continue to enjoy. The place, of course, is Disneyland, in Anaheim, California. Walt Disney World, in Orlando, Florida, became a natural (although geographically faraway) extension of Disneyland, which had become so successful.

It took the talents of thousands of people over the years to translate this one man's dreams into reality. But Walt Disney was surely the creator and monarch of his realm. Before he went to Hollywood as a young man, he had to borrow money to buy food. When he died, he was a multi-millionaire working on plans to build his own futuristic city in the swamps of Florida. This is his story.

# 2

# The Missouri Years

In Chicago on December 5, 1901, Walter Elias Disney became the fourth son of Flora and Elias Disney. Two years later, his sister, Ruth, was born.

The world of Chicago at the turn-of-the-century certainly made a big impression on America (think of all the gangster movies it inspired!), but it left no conscious memories for Walt Disney. It was not until 1906, when the family moved to Marceline, Missouri, that his remembered childhood began.

Marceline, about 120 miles (193 km) from Kansas City, was then a small community of five thousand. The horseless carriage was just making its first appearance when the Disneys arrived. The town itself was very young. It had gotten its start only nineteen years before as a stopping point on the Atcheson, Topeka and Santa Fe when that famous railroad was extended through the region. One of the engineers

*Walt, 10-months-old*

13

on the route was a favorite uncle of Walt's who often stayed at the Disney household. As a child, Walt would sometimes put his ear to the track, listening for the train that might well be bringing his uncle.

The Disneys settled not far from town on a 45 acre (18 ha) farm. Walt loved its orchards. And, as if they were not paradise enough for a small boy, just beyond their borders lay a woodland wilderness. Here, Walt and his older brother Roy spent much time together, watching closely the ways of rabbits, foxes, opossums, and raccoons. The two boys were more than brothers; they were close friends.

There was little time for such leisure activities, however. Most often, there were cows to be milked, chickens and pigs to be fed, or molasses to be made. The Disneys would trade their molasses for other needed items at the grocery store in town. Flora Disney also made butter and sold it there.

Alone on the farm one day, Walt and his sister came upon a barrel of tar. "An excellent paint," thought Walt. "Let's paint the house!" he suggested. Ruth pointed out that the tar might not come off. "Oh sure it will," said Walt with the cheery confidence that would one day win over doubtful bankers and corporation executives. Under his direction, the two dipped sticks into the tar and decorated the side of the house. Walt's "first attempt at art," as the family came to refer to the black and white mural, could still be seen from the main road when they moved away several years later.

Walt did not go to school until he was seven. In this he was not unusual. In those days, in rural areas especially, the younger children were expected to help with the family work during the day, while the older children went to school. However, Walt's mother was teaching him to read at home.

When he did begin school, his grades were unremarkable. He found a number of competing pleasures lurking outside of school. One of these was the new movie theater that had just come to Marceline. With only a hanging bedsheet for a screen, the place was probably not impressive. But in the first decade of the century, movies themselves were impressive; they were a brand-new experience—not only for children, but for everyone.

Today, people often wait until a movie appears on television or video to see it. But back then there was no television or video. When as a child Walt Disney first stole into Marceline's movie-house darkness, he may as well have stumbled into the cave of Ali Baba and the forty thieves. It was a place of unlimited treasure.

Drawing was the other magnet pulling Walt away from his studies. He enjoyed working with the pads and crayons that an aunt kept him supplied with. When Ruth came down with the measles, nine-year-old Walt entertained her by making a flip book: a series of drawings that appeared to move when the pages of the pad on which they were drawn were quickly flipped. If you flip this book that you are reading from back to front and look at the bottom right hand corners of the right hand pages, you will see an example of a flip book. Like animation, the flip book works on the principle of "persistence of vision"—the idea that the eye will be tricked into seeing motion if still drawings of figures in slightly different poses are presented to it in rapid succession. Such books made their first appearance in the nineteenth century.

Soon Walt had little time for such pleasures. Running a 45 acre (18 ha) prairie farm was hard work. Nature frequently did not cooperate; one year a drought nearly ruined the Disneys. Later, in 1909, Walt's dad came down with typhoid fever, followed by pneumonia. His two eldest sons had since gone their separate ways. It was up to Flora and 16-year-old Roy to keep things going. Walt and Ruth, both still children, were their only help.

Elias Disney recovered, but he knew that farming was no longer for him. Once again, he decided to move his family.

15

# Coming of Age

In 1910, the Disneys moved to Kansas City. This was no quiet farming town, but a bustling city of its time. It had trolleys and automobiles, theaters and movie houses. Just two blocks from the Disneys' new home, an amusement park offered itself. But like the toys in shop windows, it had to be resisted by the Disney children, for lack of money.

To support his family, Elias had become the distributor for a number of the city's newspapers, and for the next six years, Walt and Roy had to deliver the morning and evening papers. This meant waking up at 3:30 A.M., for Elias would not tolerate the conventional method of flinging papers onto porches from a moving bicycle. Instead, he demanded that each one be placed behind the porch door of the subscriber's home, so the papers wouldn't blow away, and with them the family's paltry fortune.

Even in midwestern blizzards with snowdrifts as tall as Model T's, the two brothers went twice daily on their appointed rounds. They were not even paid since their father didn't feel he owed them anything, although Elias did pay other boys three dollars a week to do the same work. In

1912, Roy, then 19 and eager to make his own way, left home. Walt, being younger, remained at home.

Although his report cards were certainly no proof of it, Walt was learning a great deal. He discovered the local library, where he read the books of Mark Twain, Robert Louis Stevenson, Sir Walter Scott, and Charles Dickens during the few hours he was not at school or at work.

You might think that at least Walt's grades in art were noteworthy. They weren't. The problem here wasn't a lack of imagination, but, in the opinion of his teachers, too much of it. One day, for example, the assignment was to sketch a bowl of flowers. Walt's flowers were of no real variety, for he had given them human faces and their leaves hands and feet. When he presented his finished botanical fantasy, his teacher scolded him for not following the assignment!

Walter Pfeiffer was a friend Walt made at school in Kansas City. They both loved "the theater," by which they meant vaudeville. This was a type of variety show that has disappeared in America, with the possible exception of the circus. But back in the days when Walt was growing up, most cities and towns had a theater where almost any night of the week you could see a vaudeville show, in which comedy, animal, musical, and acrobatic acts quickly followed one another. And once in a while, there would be an amateur night. On such occasions, ordinary people with a desire to entertain could, if they were lucky, go onstage.

Unlike Elias Disney, Walter Pfeiffer's father adored vaudeville. He encouraged the two boys to make up their own routines and to audition for a local amateur night. They did and called their act "The Two Walts."

They worked very hard on their performance. Walt rehearsed even as he delivered the newspapers that were as unavoidable as daybreak. He must have been a strange sight, pantomiming his way through the route, gesturing to bushes or the thin air. But it relieved the usual tedium of the

17

work and that of his other part-time jobs as well: delivering prescriptions for a pharmacy and selling more newspapers on a Kansas City street corner. He even began to think of a career in the theater.

Such thoughts, and even his rehearsing, were part of a secret life his family knew nothing about. Walt felt sure that his stern-looking father did not appprove of foolish entertainment such as vaudeville. As it turned out, though, it was one of those cases in which children misjudge their parents, thinking them more serious and disapproving than they really are. The proof came after the amateur night in question had come and gone.

One evening Elias was treating his wife and daughter to a show. In the middle of it, it was announced that in the next act a performer would balance three chairs on his head with a boy on top of them. The boy was Walt! In later years everyone agreed that it was impossible to say who was more surprised to see whom that night!

Walt enjoyed performing and took advantage of every opportunity to display his acting talent. While in the fifth grade, he honored Lincoln's Birthday by raiding Elias' wardrobe for a derby, transformed by cardboard into a stovepipe hat, and a long church-coat. With these and some additional hair applied to his face, Walt went off to school where he did an impersonation of Lincoln that impressed everyone. In fact, thereafter on Lincoln's Birthday every year until he was graduated, Walt was hauled from class to class by the principal to give the Gettysburg Address in this get-up.

When he was a teenager, performing still seemed a fine thing to Walt, but he began to enjoy drawing cartoons even more. Some of his earliest caricatures—drawings that exaggerated the unique features of the person being drawn— were displayed at the neighborhood barber shop. And the drawings he did at school had always made his classmates, if not his teachers, laugh. At the age of fourteen, he talked

*Walt Disney serving in the Red Cross,
in 1919, in France. Notice his cartoon
drawing on the side of the ambulance.*

his father into letting him take Saturday morning classes at the Kansas City Art Institute. A cartoonist was what he would be.

Elias also made a career decision. He was going to abandon the newspaper distributing business in favor of a new enterprise: a jelly factory back in Chicago. The family would have to relocate again. But Walt and Roy, who had recently returned home, stayed in Kansas City for one more season. Walt had already lined up a summer job selling snacks to railroad passengers. He was looking forward to a profitable and pleasant time.

Profitable it was not, at least in the strictest sense. Walt wound up having to pay for the empty soda bottles that weren't returned by customers and for snacks stolen from the box where he kept them. By the end of the summer, he was just about breaking even. But riding the trains all day through half a dozen states and exploring their towns by night was a rich experience, and Walt counted it among his happiest summers.

Later, in 1917, he rejoined the other Disneys. He took a part-time job in the jelly factory to help out with the family's earnings. But the best times of that year were the nights of his classes at the Chicago Institute of Art.

Walt desperately wanted to join the Armed Forces during World War I, but he was too young. In 1918, however, he got the chance to serve in France as a driver in the Ambulance Corps which was run by the American Red Cross to help deal with the aftermath of the war. It was a year that Walt would treasure. He made friends, saw a good deal of France, and spent lots of time drawing. He even decorated the side of his ambulance with cartoons. When he returned home, his family found him more mature. He was also more determined than ever to become a professional artist. Confidently, he announced that he was again departing, this time to become a political cartoonist for the *Kansas City Star*.

# 4

## The Kansas City Films

Walt didn't land a job with the *Star* or any other newspaper. But what did happen to him in Kansas City seems, looking back in time, to have the stamp of fate.

Walt was hired to do some drawings for an advertising firm. There he became friends with another eighteen-year-old: an artist and engineering genius with the strange name of Ubbe Iwerks. The job lasted only a short time, and soon Walt was working for another firm, the Kansas City Film Ad Company. This group made minute-long animated commercials, which, in the days before television, were shown in local movie-houses.

The animation being done here was very crude. The figures in the ads were paper cut-outs. Their joints were moved a bit at a time, then photographed after each change in position to give the illusion of movement. Walt absorbed everything he could learn about the process from those who worked in the studio. But still he wanted to know more.

He especially wanted to learn how the quality of the motion could be improved to appear more life-like. As a first step, he scoured the local library for books that might help.

21

*A drawing done by Walt when he was a teenager.*

There he found Eadweard Muybridge's classic photographic studies: *Animals in Motion* and *Humans in Motion*, books which are still used by professional animators today.

Next he talked his brother Roy, now also living in Kansas City, into helping him rig up a little studio in his garage. Finally, Walt persuaded his friend Ub, formerly Ubbe, to work with him. Deep into the nights together, they delved into the mysteries of camera and light. Their goal was to develop smoother-looking animation.

Walt also began a film of his own. When he'd completed 300 feet (91 m) of it—about three minutes—he took it to the Newman Theatre Company, which owned three movie-houses in Kansas City. The manager liked what he saw and agreed to purchase three more one-minute films when they were completed. Walt called them Newman Laugh-O-Grams.

These films were about current local events, and because of them Walt became a bit of a celebrity in Kansas City. But it wasn't enough for him. Now that he understood animation better, he wanted to use it to tell stories. He particularly wanted to tell the kinds of stories that had been entertaining people for centuries: those told, for the most part, at the fireside on long winter nights. He particularly wanted to make these tales in some way his own. He would snip here, add there, and become the tailor of tales for a new age.

*Little Red Riding Hood* was the first story to experience the Disney touch. When the film was completed, Walt quit his day job at the advertising firm and convinced Ub Iwerks to quit his. Then, with fifteen thousand dollars which they raised through contributions from local investors, they set up their own company, called Laugh-O-Gram Films. The plan was to make more animated fairy tale films to sell to theaters.

They soon found a film distributor in New York, who

23

gave them a hundred-dollar deposit and a contract to buy a series of six seven-minute films, including *Little Red Riding Hood*, for eleven thousand dollars. Walt and his new staff were overjoyed by the prospect and immediately began making films based on *Jack and the Beanstalk*, *Goldilocks and the Three Bears*, *Puss in Boots*, *Cinderella*, and *The Four Musicians of Bremen*.

By this time, Walt was producing "cel animation." This meant that his cartoons were being made in the manner introduced in 1915 by Earl Hurd, of the Bray-Hurd Process Company, and used in all the big studios.

Hurd's idea was to use paper only for creating the different backgrounds of a cartoon, since these remained still while the characters moved in the foreground. The moving characters, on the other hand, he painted on thin sheets of nitrate celluloid. Being transparent, these could be placed as needed above the painted background, and when the two layers of artwork were photographed together, they looked like one composition on the screen. This method saved the animators the labor of having to re-create the same background every time they drew a character for a cartoon.

A major problem with this system was that nitrate celluloid was a highly flammable material. A careless smoker could watch weeks of studio work, if not the whole studio, go up in flames in a moment. Eventually, sheets of non-flammable cellulose acetate replaced those made of nitrate and animation became a much safer occupation. Even today the sheets of acetate are known as "cels," which is short for cellulose.

In large studios, the process of cartoon-making had become a series of steps performed by specialists. The animators did drawings on paper of all the most important poses of the characters as they moved from one position to another. The animators were assisted by people who did drawings, also on paper, of the poses in between the key

24

Left: *Michael Sporn,
the head artist for
the animated film*
The Hunting of the
Snark *(whose draw-
ings appear on the
pages of this book).*
Above left: *animated
film artists at work,
and, at the above right,
an artist holding
a storyboard which
describes the story
sequence and char-
acter movement.*

ones. These people became known as "in-betweeners." Onto the sheets of acetate, all of these drawings—those done by the animators and the in-betweeners—were traced in ink by another group of people called "inkers." The characters were filled in with paint by people called "opaquers" or "painters." Traditionally, the inkers and painters were women, who worked for far lower wages than the others, and in a separate room away from the, mostly male, animators.

Animation paper and cels usually measure 9 x 12 inches (23 x 31 cm) and are punched so that they have two or three holes at the bottom. These holes allow the sheets of paper and cels to fit snugly onto the animator's special drawing board. This is a table equipped with a round plate of glass at its center, directly above the pegs holding the paper and cels in place. The glass can be turned completely around so that the animator can easily work on any part of the drawing without himself having to move into an awkward position.

A light bulb placed directly below the glass allows animators to trace those parts of one drawing that will remain the same in the next. It also enables them to make slight changes of pose from one drawing so that these occur in the right places. If the artists couldn't control the alignment of drawings, a character's arms or legs or entire body would be randomly moving about the screen.

At the Disney studio, as elsewhere, once the drawings were completed, traced, and inked, they had to be photographed. The artwork—that is, the transparent cels of the characters placed over their background so as to look like one layer—was put on a table below the animation camera. This was basically a motion picture camera that had been fixed to take one exposure at a time. It hung from an iron framework and pointed down at the artwork.

Film goes through a projector at twenty-four frames per second. Most people, except good animators, cannot tell if a drawing is on the screen for one frame or two. Therefore, most animation drawings are photographed for two frames, not one. The procedure is to put the first cels in a sequence of action over their background under the camera. The camera clicks as it photographs the set-up twice. Then the cel layer is removed and replaced by the next in the sequence. Click, click. And so on until a new background is also required, and that, too, must be changed. This process is repeated thousands of times in the filming of even a seven-minute cartoon.

The Kansas City cartoon company was *very* young. Walt, its president, was then twenty years old. The artists he hired were mostly teenagers. Because they were young, and because they loved animation and the excitement of being part of a new enterprise, they worked many additional hours, often with no extra pay. When they received only half their paychecks because the company's funds were low, they didn't complain. They knew that payment for a completed film could be a long time in coming.

But months after the six finished fairy tale cartoons had been shipped to New York, their distributor went bankrupt. The studio never received more than the original hundred dollar deposit for the films. Everyone, including Ub, had to find other work. Walt, living alone in the rented studio, found himself eating on credit at a nearby restaurant.

Just when it seemed to him that the future of his company was doubtful indeed, a genie appeared in the form of a neighborhood dentist. He was looking for someone to make a short animated cartoon about dental care for a local clinic. *Tommy Tucker's Tooth* filled the large hole in the company's finances, and Walt was able to hire back some of the young artists to work on it. When the film was completed, he was looking forward to his next project: *Alice's Wonderland.*

Walt had in mind a film in which a real little girl would

27

have adventures in a cartoon landscape. His idea of combining live action with animation was not an original one.

In 1921, the Fleischer Studio in New York City started a series called "Out of the Inkwell." In these films, the producer, Max Fleischer, would be shown interacting with Koko, a cartoon clown who would pop out of a real inkwell and run about an animation drawing board. Walt's idea involved reversing the roles of cartoon and real characters. He wrote to Margaret Winkler, the New York distributor of the Fleischer cartoons, describing his plans. Her repsonse was enthusiastic. Encouraged, Walt set out to make his first Alice cartoon.

But when the production's funds were spent, the film was only half-finished and the local investors refused to advance more money. As a result, the infant company went bankrupt. Walt ate cold beans out of a can, and this time no genie appeared to rescue him. He decided it was time to leave Kansas City.

The obvious place to go was New York City, the hub of the nation's cartoon industry. This industry had been born there when the great newspaper comic strip artist Winsor McCay began to make his extraordinary animated films. McCay used the most famous of these, *Gertie, the Trained Dinosaur* (1914), in a vaudeville act. Onstage he would give commands to the projected Gertie, who would charmingly respond on cue.

The film industry could not support McCay's uneconomical methods of production, and the standard of excellence he achieved in animation temporarily ended with his career. In the meantime, though, other cartoon studios had sprung up in New York, giving a host of newspaper and magazine comic strip characters life on the screen. At Pat Sullivan's studio, for example, Otto Messmer was animating the very popular Felix the Cat. The Krazy Kat Studio made films starring Krazy Kat and Ignatz Mouse. The J.R. Bray Studio films

28

featured a character called Col. Heeza Liar. Max and Dave Fleischer made cartoons with Koko, the Clown, and later Betty Boop. And Paul Terry's studio was making Farmer Al Falfa cartoons with their army of skinny mice forever on the run.

But Walt did not head for New York. Instead, he bought a one-way train ticket to California. The American West had always been a magnet for those seeking success. And by the early 1920's, it had attracted the movie industry, or at least the live-action branch of it, which had also begun in New York. Here the dependable southern California sun made it possible to shoot outdoors almost any day of the year.

Walt thought it was too late to establish himself in the New York cartoon industry not having gotten in on it at its beginning. And after owning his own studio, he didn't want to work as an employee of another. But he was broke and needed a job. His thoughts turned to his second love. He'd enjoyed being a theater performer and thought he would now become a film actor, perhaps eventually a live-action film director. This might have been enough to set him on the road to Hollywood. But there was something else. Roy, who had all along been helping Walt out with small checks from his veteran's pay, was now hospitalized for tuberculosis in Los Angeles. And their Uncle Robert lived in Los Angeles as well. Perhaps, thought Walt, Uncle Robert could be persuaded to put him up until he got his first big break.

With a heart full of hope, forty dollars in his wallet—all the money he had in the world—a suitcase holding one shirt, two pairs each of socks and underwear, and some drawing materials with which to entertain himself on the ride, he boarded the train for California.

# 5

# Hollywood

Even back in 1923 it was tough to break into a major Hollywood movie studio. Walt couldn't get work, even as a low-paid extra—an actor used in crowd scenes. And in that year there were no cartoon studios in Hollywood for him to go to. To make matters worse, Uncle Robert kept hinting that it was time for his guest to get a job.

Finally, Walt was forced to admit that his chances of becoming a movie actor were slim. If he was going to enter the wonderland of the Hollywood film business, it would have to be through a door to which he already had the key. The door was animation. The key was his experience.

Walt thought again of the Alice project, the series of films he had hoped to make in Kansas City about a little girl in a cartoon landscape. Mustering all his confidence, he poured it into a letter to Margaret Winkler, the New York distributor who had encouraged him in the past. He hoped to convince her to invest in a series of Alice films to be made in Hollywood at his brand-new studio, which, of course, did not yet exist. But Walt's excitement was contagious, even by letter. The woman responded with a contract.

30

"We're in business!" exclaimed Walt, gaily breaking the news to his brother Roy at his hospital bedside.

This had a dramatic effect on Roy. He left the hospital the next morning, feeling there was no time to lose in helping Walt to set up his new studio. An office had to be found and rented, desks ordered, artists hired. And they would need secretarial help. For this job, the brothers calculated they could pay only fifteen dollars a week. A friend suggested a young woman named Lillian Bounds for the job, since she lived within walking distance of the studio and, therefore, wouldn't need to pay carfare out of the small salary.

Walt had promised himself when he first arrived in California that he wouldn't marry until he had saved ten thousand dollars. He had barely a fraction of that when he discovered that he very much liked Lillian Bounds, the new studio's secretary. They began to see each other after working hours, but Walt couldn't bring himself to enter her house: he didn't own a suit, which he felt was a necessary item for meeting her parents. Finally, he appealed to Roy, who managed their finances. Roy agreed that the garment must be purchased. In later years, Lilly recalled that Walt was so pleased with it that he just about greeted her parents for the first time by asking: "How do you like my new suit?"

Walt and Lilly were married on July 13, 1925. Soon afterwards, Lilly stopped working at the studio. The Disneys had two daughters: Diane, born in 1933, and Sharon, in 1936. Walt and Lilly preferred to keep their home life a private matter, and so it largely remained.

Meanwhile, Walt waited for the film contract. When the Winkler contract came through, Walt convinced his old friend Ub Iwerks to leave Kansas City to join him at his new California studio. Ub was the master draftsman. Walt was the master storyteller. Roy was the one with the head for

business matters. Together, Walt felt, they made a great team.

Though it took a lot of work, the new company produced fifty-six Alice films, all on shoestring budgets. They were not very good and certainly no competition for Felix the Cat. But by 1926 both the series and the studio were firmly established. Then, Walt knew that his first series had run its course and that something new was needed. A distributor suggested he do completely animated films with a rabbit as his lead character.

In this way Oswald, the Lucky Rabbit, came about. Unlike a dozen other Disney cartoon creations, Oswald is one that few people today remember, or have even heard of. But in the 1920's Oswald was quite a popular character. What then happened to him?

The answer is that although Walt's studio had designed Oswald, it did not "own" the right to reproduce him. The distributor had that right, although Walt didn't realize it when he was making the cartoons. The distributor, seeing the success of the films, thought he could make more money from future Oswald cartoons by eliminating Walt from the process so that he wouldn't have to pay him his share of the profits. All he had to do was to lure away the Disney artists who drew the rabbit by promising them somewhat higher pay. They could go on making the films for him directly. This is exactly what happened.

Someone else might have despaired, but not Walt. He realized he still had the key to Oswald's success: his own creative talent. Since no one could take *that* away, he felt that there was every reason to be confident about the future. But he had learned a lesson he would never forget. In the future he made sure that he legally owned *forever* the rights to all his creations. And in a way, the loss of Oswald was directly responsible for the birth of that most famous Disney legacy—Mickey Mouse.

32

Mickey Mouse is full of human qualities. Most often he's mischievous and merry. But he can also be brave, smart, cruel, or tender. We see him as a mountaineer, a theater manager, an orchestra conductor, a vacationer, a pilot, a sportsman, a shipbuilder. Like children with imagination, he is anything he wants to be.

Walt and Ub both contributed to Mickey's creation. In the early days, Walt provided Mickey's voice as well as most of the stories in the cartoons. Ub animated Mickey, therefore giving him much of his personality.

The first Mickey Mouse cartoon was a short called *Plane Crazy*. It was inspired by Charles Lindbergh's heroic flight during that year. Audiences seemed to like the cartoon, but they weren't wildly enthusiastic about it.

Walt was not discouraged by its luke-warm reception. In fact, he was all fired up about something new. Sound films had only recently been introduced, and Walt was one of those who saw the future in the technological breakthrough. The animation for two more Mickey cartoons—*Gallopin' Gaucho* and *Steamboat Willie*—were already complete, but Walt didn't want to wait any longer to release a sound film. So off he went to New York with the print of *Steamboat Willie* in hand, to record the music for a soundtrack. This had to be done twice, because the first time the orchestra conductor paid no attention to Walt's system of timing the music to the actions and, instead, relied on his own ability to conduct the musicians while watching the film. The result was that the music was out of synch with the action, which, of course, ruined all the effects, and the whole film.

The second recording went perfectly. *Steamboat Willie* was launched in theaters around the country, and with it the career of Mickey Mouse. The film was billed as "the first animated sound cartoon." That claim was not absolutely accurate. The Fleischers had been producing their "Song Car-Tunes," beginning in 1924 with *Oh, Mabel.* The pur-

33

pose of these films was to assist in movie-audience "sing-alongs," at the time a popular form of entertainment. On the screen would appear the printed words of a popular song, and the whole movie audience would sing it. To keep people singing in time, the Fleischers introduced an animated "bouncing ball," which indicated when it was time to sing the next word. Traditionally, the theater organist had provided the musical accompaniment. But the Fleischers also introduced a soundtrack that provided a musical background and sound effects.

Still, it was Walt Disney who, from the very beginning, was to make the fullest use of sound in cartoons. *Steamboat Willie* was the first cartoon with synchronized sound. Disney recognized the capacity of the soundtrack to add humor to what was happening on the screen. Even today, *Steamboat Willie* is fun to watch, not so much because of what Mickey does, but because of the way his antics are punctuated by the soundtrack. In fact, for a first effort in sound cartoons, *Steamboat Willie* is crammed with music and sound effects, from the parrot gurgling his words when a pail of water lands on his head to Minnie Mouse's high heel shoes clacking musically as she runs along the riverbank.

The climax comes when a goat swallows sheet music to the song "Turkey in the Straw" and Mickey get the idea of cranking his tail, thereby turning the animal into a living music box that "plays" the song. Mickey then one-ups this effect several times by adding more and more layers of musical accompaniment to the song. He achieves his unique orchestration by playing, in turn, a garbage pail, a washboard, the tails of suckling piglets (making them squeal in different pitches by pulling their tails), the neck of a duck, and the teeth of a cow with xylophone hammers! In this cartoon the whole world, it seems, is an array of potential musical instruments. It was this wonderfully inventive and

34

*Mickey Mouse in "Steamboat Willie," the first cartoon with synchronized sound. The movie first appeared at the Colony Theatre on November 18, 1928. This date is considered Mickey Mouse's birthday.*

rich use of sound that made Mickey the sensation he was, beginning with *Steamboat Willie.*

The coming of sound made the filmmaking business far more complicated than it had been. To make a good sound cartoon, much time had to be spent with the composer working out the details of just how the music would fit into each sequence. Walt was now determined that his cartoons be the best. He realized that this required teamwork, time, and the best equipment available.

So he organized his artists into teams. An experienced animator would work closely with an assistant and an in-betweener, the person who drew the poses in between the most important ones. Unlike the situation at other cartoon studios, each team had its own workroom equipped with a moviola. This is a small projector designed to run a reel of film in its rough, unfinished stage and separately from the soundtrack. With it, animators could see at any time during the production how their animation was coming along, even if it was still just film of their pencil drawings on paper. Studying the movement of characters while they were still at this stage was called "pencil-testing."

At the other studios, where there was usually only one moviola, animators never saw their work until the whole film was completed. A moviola was—and still is—an expensive piece of equipment. But Walt spared no expense when it came to technology that would improve his films. He encouraged his staff to experiment, to do pencil-tests. That, he knew, took time. And unlike rival cartoon producers, he did not require any daily or weekly minimum amount of finished work from his artists.

Walt was also unique among cartoon producers in another way. Many animators of that time hadn't had the opportunity to receive formal art education. Walt encouraged his staff to study fine art after working hours. In the earliest days, he drove his animators to classes at the nearby Choui-

36

nard Art Institute. In the 1930's, he hired one of its teachers, Don Graham, to give evening classes right at the studio.

There were classes in life drawing—that is, from live models—as well as lectures on famous old artists, and on theories of movement and how they could be applied to animation. Other times, the class would analyze the movements of great comic actors like Charlie Chaplin by slowing the film down so that they could study frame by frame what was happening. It was an exciting time for the artists who worked at the Disney studio in those years, for it was a place fiercely devoted to learning.

By 1935, the art courses were costing the studio more than $100,000. How could the Disneys afford them when other cartoon studios couldn't afford even a second moviola? The answer is that the profits of the Disney studio didn't come entirely from films. Much of the money came from companies that made products ranging from wrist watches to pastry. These companies had one thing in common: they paid the Disney studio to use a picture of a character, like Mickey Mouse, to sell their products.

It began one day in 1930, when Walt was stopped in the lobby of a New York hotel by a man who asked if he could put a picture of Mickey Mouse on the school notebooks he sold if he gave Walt three hundred dollars. Walt hastily signed the contract the man stuck in front of him. The incident made the Disneys realize that here was an as-yet untapped source of profits available to them. Over the years, millions of dollars poured into the studio from companies around the world licensed to sell items bearing the image of a Disney character.

By 1929, Mickey Mouse had fan clubs across America, and the demand for more of his films grew. Walt responded by featuring his star in shorts throughout the 1930's. Probably the best of these is *The Band Concert.*

In this film, Mickey is a conductor of a band at a park concert. Donald Duck, here seen in one of his earliest screen performances, is a heckler who continually frustrates the attempts of Mickey and the band members—including the lovers Clarabelle Cow and Horace Horsecollar on flute—to play the piece they have begun. But the band succeeds despite the combined forces of a sudden tornado and the mischievous Duck. It doesn't matter that the musicians play the last chord while each is hanging from a different branch of a tree. Till the last note, they have miraculously managed to keep in time and in tune. We, the real audience, feel they have triumphed, though the cartoon audience has long since fled.

Walt made this film in 1935 to make people laugh. But the cartoon is also a reminder that to be excellent in music, film, or anything else, you need great determination. In its funny way, *The Band Concert* is a tribute to the human spirit, a film to live by.

Even as the first Mickey cartoons were gathering steam, Walt wanted to try a different cartoon style. So he began a new series of shorts, which he called "Silly Symphonies."

*The Skeleton Dance* (1929) was the first of the "Silly Symphonies." Theater managers were at first uncertain about showing a film in which a bunch of skeletons get out of their graves and do a dance to a piece of classical music. Too depressing, they said. But audiences disagreed, for the music seemed to fit each action so perfectly that seeing it was like watching a perfectly performed and funny ballet.

*Flowers and Trees* was another, about a male tree desperately in love with a female tree. What made it special to the audiences that saw it in 1932 was that it was in Technicolor, and therefore like no other film—live-action or cartoon—that they had ever seen. The invention of three-strip Technicolor made vividly colored films possible for the first time. But the process was not ready for use in live-action

At the Walt Disney Studios in Hollywood
during the 1930s, Mickey Mouse cartoons
and the "Silly Symphonies" were created.

film in 1932. Walt wanted to be the first to use it, but because of the great expense, Roy was against the idea. Finally, Walt went to the makers of Technicolor and convinced them that, if he purchased it from them, they should grant him two years for its exclusive use in short cartoons. Surprisingly, they agreed, and so for two years Disney cartoons were the only ones in full color. *Flowers and Trees* also became the first cartoon ever to win an Academy Award.

In 1933, *Three Little Pigs*, the thirty-sixth Silly Symphony, became an instant hit. It was a cartoon that spoke to America, and not only its children. When adults first viewed *Three Little Pigs*, they saw in the wolf a symbol of the Depression.

Like the wolf, the Great Depression of the 1930's, with its high unemployment rate, was a source of dread and fear to most citizens. Movie-goers cheered when the wolf got his punishment, and the playful theme song, "Who's Afraid of the Big Bad Wolf?" became a hit.

Many of the Disney shorts of the 1930's successfully entertained theater audiences. But now even the best of them can be seen as the sketches of an artist who longed for a larger canvas.

For a long time, Walt had wanted to make a cartoon feature, a film seventy-five minutes or more in length as compared with shorts, which were usually seven minutes long. Walt felt that in a feature he would be able to tell a story properly. There would be time to develop characters and plot. He also saw that the economics of the movie business was making features the way of the future. Theaters were now offering "the double feature" as a way of attracting larger audiences. As a result, they were renting fewer shorts as "filler."

Walt chose *Snow White and the Seven Dwarfs* for his first feature. On an evening in 1934, he gathered around him his best animators and story people and acted out the story as he saw it in his mind from start to finish. The story-telling took three hours, for he played every part and included many details.

The film would cost one-and-a-half-million dollars to make, money that would have to be borrowed from a bank. If the project failed, the bank would get the studio, the film, and both Roy and Walt's homes. Lilly and Roy were firmly against the idea. But as so often happened when Walt was possessed by an idea, he dazzled its opponents with his visions until he won out.

# 6

# The Early Features

If you had visited the Disney studio on a day in 1935, you could have seen many curious sights. In fact, had it been raining, even before you stepped inside, you might have seen some strange behavior: for example, someone squatting on the ground intently studying a puddle as it was being formed. It would have been one of the people assigned to the studio's "special effects" unit. This group was in charge of creating the most realistic-looking rain, lightning, fog, and mist ever seen in animation. The effects were needed in the forest sequences of *Snow White*.

Inside the studio, you might have run into a parade of small people and costumed actors. Although *Snow White and the Seven Dwarfs* was to be a fully animated film, it did rely on human actors for more than the voices. The animation of some of the characters was done by a technique called *rotoscoping*, which was used as early as 1915 by the Fleischer studio.

This method involved first filming actors going through a particular motion—a dance, for example. The film was then put into a machine that projected the sequence one frame at a time. Someone then had to trace each exposure from the film onto animation paper. These drawings traced directly from film served as guides for the animators who did the final drawings of the cartoon characters going through the same motions as the actors. The effect of rotoscoping on the screen is more flowing, human-like movement than is usual in cartoons.

*Snow White and the Seven Dwarfs* (1937), the first American feature-length cartoon, was three years in production. More than 250,000 separate drawings went into the making of the film. The animators, inkers, and painters spent most of their days, and sometimes also their nights, hunched over their desks. Their work required accuracy and speed, patience and concentration.

During the making of *Snow White*, the Disney artists and technicians were a very happy work force. The space they labored in was cramped and uncomfortable, but that didn't seem to matter. The artists were happy because they knew they were the best animation crew in the country and that they were making a very special movie. They pushed forward, sometimes working round the clock with no extra pay in order to meet the deadline. They did not want the Disneys to lose the film and their studio to the Bank of America.

The premiere of *Snow White and the Seven Dwarfs* was a great social event. It was held at one of Hollywood's most posh theaters, and many famous stars turned out to see it. The film was also a huge popular success, and in 1939 it earned Walt a special Academy Award. It was presented to him by a ten-year-old movie star named Shirley Temple.

The profits from the film were large enough for Walt to begin planning additional features and to build a new and larger studio. Walt wanted the new studio to be a worker's paradise. He concerned himself with every detail of its design. Someone even found him in his office one day taking

apart a chair to see how it could be changed so that animators would be more comfortable. He wanted animators, story people, musicians, and sound technicians each to have their own space. The buildings would all be air-conditioned and surrounded by broad lawns where workers could play baseball and volleyball during lunch hour. Inside, there would be lounges, a gymnasium, restaurants, and a snack bar with delivery service to workers' desks!

While the new studio was being built, Walt's staff of employees worked hard on many projects. *Pinocchio* (1940), based on the well-known book by Carlo Collodi, was the next project on the drawing boards. It was the story of a puppet who becomes a real boy, and it presented the animators with a problem. How could people have feelings for a character made of wood? The solution was to make Jiminy Cricket, a minor figure in the book and soon crushed under Pinocchio's foot, a major—and, more importantly, a lovable—character.

The artists who worked on *Pinocchio* enjoyed the greatest use ever of the multiplane camera. Perched on an iron framework fourteen feet tall, this type of camera is able to photograph more than one layer of backgrounds at a time. To understand how this is done, imagine a pane of glass with a tree painted on it. It is placed an inch or two (2.5 or 5 cm) below the camera's lens. A second pane of glass, show-

Top: *Disney fascinated with models of the seven dwarfs.*
Bottom: *Walt Disney receiving a special Oscar award (one big, seven little—for the seven dwarfs) presented to him by Shirley Temple.*

45

ing a house, is placed several inches below the first. A third glass, depicting a mountain, is placed a few inches below the second. When all three layers are simultaneously photographed, it looks as if the tree is standing in the foreground with the house well behind it and the mountain on the horizon. In short, the lens of this camera "sees" layers of flat paintings the way the human eye sees three-dimensional objects in real space. The most dazzling use of it occurs in an early scene of *Pinocchio*.

In that scene, the audience is given a spectacular tour of Pinocchio's village. We see behind and beyond trees into streets and around their corners. We know that we are watching cartoon drawings, but for those few moments it is easy to believe that we are looking at a three-dimensional space.

The next two features, *Fantasia* (1940) and *Bambi* (1942), were very different from each other. Walt once described *Bambi* as "the love life of a little deer." It is also a serious, gripping film about life and death. The moment when young Bambi learns that his mother has been killed by hunters has a lasting effect on viewers. Even after more than forty years, adults who saw the film as children can still recall that scene and how it made them feel.

*Fantasia* began with Walt wanting to do something for his first star, whose popularity was then dwindling. Mickey Mouse had undergone a number of changes since his earliest film appearances a decade before. He was now rounder, less rodent-like, and, to some eyes, cuter—like the other Disney characters. But he was also less mischievous and more reserved, even shy. The mischievous quality that had at first made him so appealing was, to some extent, gone.

Walt's solution was to star Mickey in a short film based on an old tale called "The Sorcerer's Apprentice," for which Paul Dukas had written concert music. In the story, a sorcerer's lazy young assistant—to be played by Mickey—

46

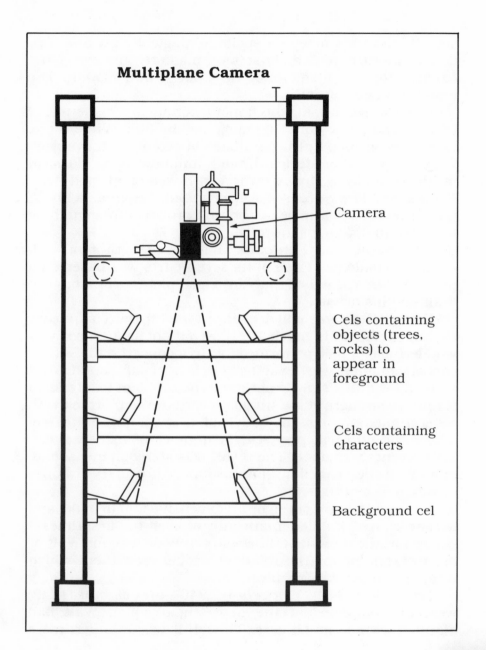

**Multiplane Camera**

Camera

Cels containing objects (trees, rocks) to appear in foreground

Cels containing characters

Background cel

secretly uses his master's spells to magically get his work done. Unfortunately, he hasn't yet mastered the spells and cannot stop the magic once he's put it into motion. The result is a near disaster.

Leopold Stokowski, the famous conductor, came to the Disney studio to record the music for the film. While there, he became excited by the possibility of extending the project. Why not tell other stories through animation and classical music alone? Why stop here? His enthusiasm infected Walt. Eventually, *The Sorcerer's Apprentice*, begun as a short, had, like Mickey's magic-dabbling, grown into something bigger than it was meant to be.

The result was *Fantasia*, a feature-length film with almost no dialogue. Each of its seven parts was based on a piece of classical music that suggested pictures or stories to Walt and his artists.

Dolby Sound was still decades in the future. That meant that music heard in movie theaters did not sound nearly as wonderful as music performed live in a concert hall. But the concert quality was exactly the quality of sound Walt wanted for *Fantasia*. He assigned the problem to a team of sound researchers at his studio. Record the soundtrack with several microphones, they advised, and equip the theaters where the film will play with a number of loudspeakers. This is what was done. The result was stereophonic sound, or as Walt then called it, "Fantasound." It was the first use of stereo in movies.

*Fantasia* turned out to be an expensive film to make and to release. And it failed financially, at least the first times it showed at theaters. Its failure did not bode well for Walt or his workers, or for the relationship between them which was then in serious trouble.

*Fantasia* (1940), *Pinocchio* (1940), and *Bambi* (1942) were all completed at the new studio which Walt had planned with so much care. Though it was a larger, more

48

comfortable space, his staff did not seem to regard it as the paradise he had imagined it would be. If anything, the workers were, for the most part, far less happy than they had been previously. It was Walt's great misfortune not to see how unhappy they were or to understand why.

By the late 1930's, the Disney studio employed over a thousand people. It was not possible to run such a large organization the way Walt had run his earlier studios with only a dozen or so employees, who were also his friends. Employees of large companies expect to be paid for all their hours of work, and when bonuses are promised, they need to be given.

This was not the case in the opinion of many workers then at the Disney studio. During the making of *Snow White*, they had labored round the clock, with no extra pay, to meet the bank's deadline. Back then, there had been promises of future bonuses if the film did well. It did extremely well, but many of the expected bonuses did not come about. Instead, the profits were poured into more expensive projects. Some of the workers were resentful, and now that the new films were doing poorly there was a general fear of lay-offs.

By 1940, attempts were being made on the West Coast to create an industry-wide union of cartoonists. The Disneys tried to persuade their workers not to join it, but to organize a union of just Disney artists. If anything, these efforts convinced some of them to join one of the new industry-wide unions.

On May 20, 1941, one such group succeeded in organizing a strike against the Disney studio. Although fewer than half the artists took part in it, the strike had a long-lasting effect. Walt felt betrayed by the striking workers, and when they returned there was tension between them and those employees who had continued working during the strike. Walt seemed unable to understand the striking workers'

49

point of view. The spirit of togetherness which had distinguished the studio during the making of *Snow White* would never completely return.

Even before the troubles were settled, Walt accepted an invitation from the U.S. Government to visit South America. It was to be a good will tour. At first he protested that he was a filmmaker, not a diplomat. But, asked the Government officials, who was more qualified to spread good will than the man who made Mickey Mouse? Walt agreed to go, provided that a film or two, to be financed by the Government, could be made in the process.

So it was that Walt and Lilly, along with a small crew, toured Chile, Argentina, Colombia, Brazil, and Bolivia. Wherever they went, people flocked to meet the creator of Mickey Mouse. Between barbecues and public appearances, the crew worked. The artists sketched the landscapes, the people, and the animals of the places they visited. The composers listened to the music of these countries. And Walt dreamed up stories. Before their return to California, two animated films were in the works: *The Three Caballeros* and *Saludos Amigos*. Both featured a new character: a cigar-smoking parrot named José Carioca.

In December 1941, shortly after the bombing of Pearl Harbor, Walt Disney received a telephone report of incredible news. The U.S. Army was taking over part of his studio! It was to be used as a 700-man anti-aircraft unit to protect defense plants in the Los Angeles area. In the parking lot, ammunition soon replaced employees' cars. In the work areas, camera equipment gave way to military equipment. And hundreds of soldiers were making themselves at home. They were to live, day and night, at the studio for the next eight months.

When the Government ceased to fear an attack on the mainland, most of these soldiers left. They were replaced, though, with other military personnel. It was decided that the studio would remain in the service of the war effort. Part of that effort involved making cartoons.

*Alice in Wonderland* (1951) and *Peter Pan* (1953), the animated features then in production, were put on hold. Immediately and for the next four years, the Disney staff was put to work on dozens of animated films for the Government and branches of the Armed Services. These ranged from films that promoted the sale of war bonds and saving certificates to training films on how to identify aircraft.

The company also made films that tried to persuade the public that the Government was making the right decisions in the war. The most famous of these was a cartoon called *Der Fuehrer's Face* (1942), in which Donald Duck dreams he is stuck in a German war-machine factory. The film mocked Nazi Germany; American audiences loved it.

Some of Walt's young artists were themselves drafted into the Armed Services. But eventually the Draft Board saw the work being done at the Disney studio as so important that these artists were permitted to remain on their jobs as a regular form of military service. They reported to their desks at the studio in uniform! There, in addition to working on the war films, they designed more than 1,200 insignia (decorative symbols) for military units.

Walt, who loved flying, was impressed by a book that appeared, called *Victory Through Air Power*. The author, Major Alexander P. de Seversky, argued that America could best win the war if it stepped up its use of fighting planes. Walt decided to adapt the book into a live-action and animated film. *Victory Through Air Power* was quickly made.

One of those who saw the film was England's Prime Minister Winston Churchill. At a key conference held to discuss the coming invasion of Europe, he asked President Franklin

51

Delano Roosevelt if *he* had seen it. The answer was no.
Then, according to historian John Gunther in his book enti-
tled *Taken at the Flood*:

> *The President and the Prime Minister saw it*
> *together that night, and Roosevelt was much*
> *excited by the way Disney's aircraft masterfully*
> *wiped ships off the seas. It was run again the*
> *next day, and then FDR invited the Joint Chiefs*
> *to have a look at it. This played an important*
> *role in the decision that was then taken to give*
> *the D-Day invasion sufficient air power.*

# 7

# New Directions

In December 1947, Walt wrote in a letter to his sister Ruth: "I bought myself a birthday/Christmas present—something I've wanted all my life—an electric train. . . . What fun I'm having! It's a freight train with a whistle and real smoke comes out of the smokestack. . . ."

Ollie Johnston, one of the animators at the Disney studio, learned of Walt's train and the pleasure he took in it. Johnston, himself, was building a one-twelfth scale model railroad. He invited Walt to his home, and the result was inevitable. Walt wanted such a railroad, too!

So he set up a machine shop, where he was soon learning how to construct wooden box cars large enough to carry human passengers. Eventually, the Disneys bought a new home with property large enough to hold the miniature railroad and its half-mile (.90-km) run. He enjoyed nothing more than putting on his engineer's cap and overalls and taking his daughters and their friends for rides.

Walt was fascinated by miniature objects of all sorts. He admired them, collected them during his travels, and made them for his railroad in the barn he used as a workshop.

53

With studio story man and production designer, Ken Anderson, he also built a series of miniature sets of old-fashioned scenes, which they then outfitted with small mechanical figures.

Walt's love of the "old-fashioned" led him to imagine a park which would have the feeling of a small, turn-of-the-century town. He thought it would do nicely on a small piece of property he owned across the street from the studio. When he finished imagining, his park required more than two hundred acres (80 ha)! It was, of course, Disneyland, which was eventually built in Anaheim, California.

The planning of the park took several years, for as time went on, Walt's plans became more and more elaborate. Eventually, a problem had to be faced: how to pay for its construction. Clearly, profits from the Disney films alone could not produce enough money.

In the decade following the War, the studio released several animated features, including *Cinderella* (1950), *Alice in Wonderland* (1951), and *Peter Pan* (1953). The Disneys had also begun to make live-action features like *Treasure Island* (1950) and *20,000 Leagues Under the Sea* (1954), as well as documentary films about wildlife. They also continued to make short cartoons, although now Mickey and his friends had serious competition from Bugs Bunny, Daffy Duck, Porky Pig, and other characters from the Warner Brothers Studio, who burst onto the screen with their zany exuberance.

The Disney output was considerable, and many of the films won awards, but they were not huge financial successes. The money for Disneyland would have to come from a source outside the studio. But where? Walt spent many sleepless nights pondering the question before the answer came to him: television.

It wasn't an obvious answer. In 1953, television was still very young. But Walt felt sure that television could make the

park in his mind a reality. The studio could produce a weekly show for families. He'd make it a condition that whichever
network sponsored it would have to invest heavily in the
park.

The plan worked. ABC-TV bought the idea, and the "Disneyland" television show proved a great success. Walt himself introduced the programs, and each week his presence in
many American living rooms was as welcome as that of a
favorite aunt or uncle. The show presented some of the old
Disney features and nature films, as well as new material.
Occasionally, there were films of the park as it was being
built, so that viewers wanted to go to Disneyland even before
its gates were open to the public.

The mini-series "Davy Crockett," a story about a frontier
woodsman during the time of the Alamo, was especially popular. People bought ten million records of the Davy Crockett
theme song and millions of Davy Crockett "coonskin" hats.
The studio had made no special plans to sell these. But boys
across the country wanted to look like Davy Crockett. When
American supplies of raccoon skins were gone because of
the great demand, manufacturers worked overtime to make
available other varieties of furry Crockett headgear.

In 1955, "The Mickey Mouse Club" began its run and
made television history. For the next two years, between
5:00 and 6:00 P.M., three-quarters of the nation's sets were
tuned in. It also ran as a half-hour show for two more years.
The show, aimed at the pre-teen audience, featured a group
of children, called Mouseketeers because of the Mickey
Mouse ears they wore on their heads. Along with two hono-
rary adult members, Jimmie Dodd and Disney cartoonist
Roy Williams, they sang, danced, and starred in serials
based on children's books. The show also presented some of
the old Disney cartoons to a generation born after the films
had been made.

The year 1955 also saw the opening of Disneyland. It

*The Mouseketeers*

was indeed Disney's land. Into its design he had poured all the things he loved most: miniatures of all kinds, mechanically operated figures, railroads, and the memories of his Missouri boyhood. In fact, Walt built a town similar to Marceline—the town where he had lived as a young boy—on a small scale, calling it Main Street, U.S.A. It is the port of entry to Disneyland, and it was Walt's favorite part of the park. He kept a furnished apartment in one of its buildings so that he could sleep over whenever he wanted to.

Walt wanted the shops on Main Street to be large enough for people to wander into and buy things, but he also wanted the overall feeling of the place to be that of a miniature. So he had the ground level shops built to full scale, but the second stories of the buildings built to 80 percent their normal size, and the third story levels to only 60 percent. As a result, when you walk down this street, you feel you are in a place that is far cosier and nicer than any real town you've been to. It is also cleaner and fresher-looking because its buildings are repainted more frequently than those of any real town. From Main Street you are led to the four regions of Disneyland: Fantasyland, Adventureland, Frontierland, and Tomorrowland.

Fantasyland, dominated by Sleeping Beauty Castle, offers rides ranging from those suitable for tots, like the cup and saucer ride inspired by the Mad Hatter's tea party in *Alice in Wonderland*, to those designed for people who aren't afraid of anything. One of the most popular attractions is "Pirates of the Caribbean." It is a long boatride through darkness in which mechanical figures enact exciting scenes in an atmosphere so realistic it even *smells* as if you're marooned in a backwater marsh. This exhibit, in fact, is said to have inspired film director Roman Polanski to make his movie *Pirates*.

Another favorite is the "Haunted Mansion," scary right from the start because the floor suddenly drops several sto-

ries when you aren't expecting it to! You then board a ride which takes you through fantastic scenes.

Disneyland also offers a number of rides for the roller-coaster addict. The dips and rises and hairpin turns of "Space Mountain," for example, produce particularly thrilling effects because, unlike those of most roller-coaster rides, they occur in the dark. Since you can't see them coming, your stomach can't anticipate them. The bobsled ride down the Matterhorn is also quite a stupendous ride at Disneyland.

For those who wish to be neither terrified nor made temporarily ill, there are the gentler rides down the Mississippi River aboard the "Mark Twain," a large-scale model of the steamboats that plied the actual river, and the "Jungle Cruise" through the Amazon River, where the most you're likely to meet up with is a mechanical alligator peering out of the water.

In a way, Disneyland is an on-going party. Food and music are never far off, and often they are found in combination. A Dixieland band is likely to be playing at an outdoor cafe in New Orleans Square, where the favorites of Creole cuisine are in ready supply.

However charming during the day, Disneyland is most dazzling after dark. Then the "Mark Twain" becomes a moving necklace of light. The rides and restaurants shimmer and twinkle, too. During the summer, there's bound to be a fireworks display, if not a full-scale parade. And a real-life Tinker Bell "flies" along a high wire to welcome the night.

Even after the opening of Disneyland, Walt's interest in the park remained high. He saw it as something he could nurture and watch grow. He explained "It's something that will never be finished, something I can keep developing . . . It's alive . . . Not only can I add things, but even the trees will keep growing."

*Disneyland, overlooking the Matterhorn ride*

Walt saw the 1964 New York World's Fair as an opportunity to add to Disneyland, to put the Disney name before the fair-going public. His idea was to create the exhibits to be sponsored by some of the nation's large corporations. Here was the chance, he thought, to create new and lively shows with the money of other companies. And when the Fair was over, these exhibits could be brought to Disneyland.

It was shrewd thinking. Three major corporations—Ford, General Electric, and Pepsi-Cola—as well as the State of Illinois were excited about having the Disney organization build their exhibits. These proved to be among the most popular pavilions at the Fair.

All of them depended upon a technology that the Disney engineers had been experimenting with for years. Called Audio-Animatronics, it involved sound, animation, and electronics. Sound impulses recorded on a magnetic tape were used to make a figure move on cue in a way that was very life-like. Movement of the figures' mouths could be hooked up to correspond with a pre-recorded soundtrack so that these figures could appear to be speaking or singing.

One of the most charming of the World's Fair exhibits was "It's a Small World," originally created for Pepsi-Cola and now permanently installed at Disneyland. Spectators took a boatride through chambers teeming with Audio-Animatronics dolls representing different countries. Seeing and hearing these hundreds of little dolls all singing the same round tended to make most people laugh.

During the 1950's and into the 1960's, the Disney studio produced dozens of family-oriented films. Some were animated features such as *Lady and the Tramp* (1955), *Sleeping Beauty* (1959), *The Sword in the Stone* (1963), and *The Jungle Book* (1967). Others were live-action features. *Old Yeller* (1957), *Darby O'Gill and the Little People* (1959), *Kidnapped* (1960), *Pollyanna* (1960), and *The*

60

*Absent-Minded Professor* (1961) are just a few titles. In 1964, the Disney studio released its most popular and financially successful film ever—the musical *Mary Poppins*, about an English nanny who could fly. This smash hit won five Academy Awards and the generous praise of film critics.

The 1960's also saw the development of CalArts or, more properly, the California Institute of the Arts. CalArts resulted from Walt's desire to save the financially distressed Chouinard Art Institute, the school that had generously provided free art classes for Disney animators in the days before the studio could afford to pay for them. Newly established CalArts would be a training ground for young artists and, Walt hoped, a source of talent that his studio could eventually draw on.

*Cinderella Castle, Walt Disney World*

# 8

## *The Last Dream*

In the ten years following its opening, Disneyland proved to be one of the great magnets of the modern world, attracting royalty as well as millions of less famous visitors each year. Originally Walt had wanted there to be only one Disneyland. But as early as 1958, plans were afoot to build another. In 1965, the Florida property for Walt Disney World was purchased. It was 27,400 acres (10,960 ha): more than a hundred times the size of Disneyland!

Walt did not want just a repeat performance; he wanted to do something new, to build a model city. It was to be something really big, not a miniature this time, but a real city. The 20,000 people who would live there would be the employees and their families of Walt Disney World. It was to be a model in this sense only: a shimmering pearl for the old, problem-riddled cities of the world to marvel at and emulate. Walt called his imagined city EPCOT. That was short for Experimental Prototype Community of Tomorrow.

"EPCOT," said Walt, "will be a living, breathing community. It will worry about pre-school education, home envi-

63

ronments, employment . . . EPCOT will be no architectural monument, but will be a showcase of what American ingenuity and technology can do."

Walt's plans called for a downtown hub with main avenues and transportation lines radiating out like the spokes of a wheel. The wedge-shaped areas between the spokes were for homes, schools, and, of course, parks. Each home would face a park. The downtown area was to be covered and completely climate-controlled. There would be no rain, cold, or humidity. In fact, there would not even be a sense of day or night.

Walt was often accused of hating cars. That was not true. But he did think they should take a back-seat, at least in cities, to human feet. EPCOT was to be a paradise for those who enjoyed walking. Cars would be limited to roadways built below street level where they could zip along without endangering or spoiling the fun of people on foot. One form of motor traffic *would* be allowed around people: mass transit. And that would be the best that imagination, combined with state-of-the-art-technology, could produce.

To make these plans a reality, Walt needed to obtain nearly total control over his huge piece of real estate. Existing building codes and zoning laws simply did not provide for the kind of innovative building he intended to do. But once again, Walt was able to get his way because his enthusiasm for the project rubbed off on those in power. Eventually, Florida authorities granted him an unusual degree of control over the swamp he saw as the real Tomorrowland.

Walt Disney was now getting older, and for many months he had been suffering with cancer. Death robbed him of the chance to see his plans for EPCOT through. But even during his final days in a hospital bed, he talked of EPCOT. On December 15, 1966, Walt Disney died.

Though the plans for this futuristic city, as Disney had envisioned it, were not to be fulfilled, the seeds of Walt's last

*EPCOT Center opened in 1982. The mono-rail (mass transit) moves along tracks above-ground. Behind it is Spaceship Earth, the world's largest geosphere, a structural form in the shape of a sphere.*

dream can be found in Walt Disney World. Nearby, EPCOT Center was built, but as an exhibition center, not a city. Unfortunately, Walt did not live to see its opening.

The Florida park has since been seen by some of America's most respected architects and town planners as a bold experiment in urban design. What they find revolutionary about Walt Disney World lies below ground, the part that tourists never see. Here, amid fluorescent-lit, cinder-blocked-lined tunnels, those in charge of repair in the vast park have access to all of the electrical lines that service it. But there is much more than pipes and wires, ducts and cables, and computer boards down in the basement. There is a pneumatic tube network that speeds bags of garbage at 60 miles an hour to a compacting station located some distance away. Also traveling through the tunnel are electric carts bearing supplies to and from distant warehouses. Walt Disney World is also a model of anti-pollution technology and attitudes. For example, there is the 100-acre (40-ha) "Living Farm," where plants and trees are used to recycle waste water into clean water.

Walt did not want his new park to oust the non-human tenants of the land. So he set aside about a third of the woodland acreage of Walt Disney World as a preserve. Birds, fish, bears, and alligators remain here in their swampy homes, undisturbed by tourists, for whom the site is strictly off-limits. The only humans allowed in are those doing serious studies in ecology and conservation.

It was a long way from a silent cartoon called *Plane Crazy*, with Mickey Mouse as a barn-storming pilot, to plans for Walt Disney World, that included EPCOT. If the two have a common message, it is this: you *can* do the seemingly impossible.

In some ways, Walt Disney's life as well as his works were proof of this message. No one would have predicted that the Missouri boy who couldn't make a dime all summer selling snacks on the Santa Fe would eventually become a multi-millionaire whose name would be known worldwide. But he did. It was due to a combination of perseverance, hard work, luck, and the drive to create a perfect place that he could share with the world.

# *Further Reading*

Canemaker, John. *The Animated Raggedy Ann and Andy: An Intimate Look at the Art of Animation, Its History, Techniques, and Artists.* Indianapolis, Indiana: Bobbs-Merrill, 1977.

_____. *Treasures of Disney Animation Art.* New York: Abbeville Press, 1982.

Crafton, Donald. *Before Mickey.* Cambridge, Massachusetts: The M.I.T. Press, 1982.

Di Franco, Jo Ann. *Walt Disney: When Dreams Come True.* Minneapolis, Minnesota: Dillon Press, 1985.

Finch, Christopher. *The Art of Walt Disney.* New York: Abrams, 1973.

Laybourne, Kit. *The Animation Book.* New York: Crown, 1979.

Maltin, Leonard. *The Disney Films.* New York: Crown, 1984.

Montgomery, Elizabeth Rider. *Walt Disney: Master of Make-Believe.* Champaign, Illinois: Garrard Publishing, 1971.

Schickel, Richard. *The Disney Version.* New York: Simon and Schuster, 1985.

Thomas, Bob. *The Art of Animation: The Story of the Disney Contributions to a New Art.* New York: Simon and Schuster, 1958.

_____. *Walt Disney: An American Original.* New York: Simon and Schuster, 1976.

Thomas, Frank, and Johnston, Ollie. *Disney Animation: The Illusion of Life.* New York: Abbeville Press, 1984.

# *Index*

72